THE ALLIS FAMILY; OR, SCENES OF WESTERN LIFE

by American Sunday School Union

New edition and formatting

Based on Public Domain Text

Copyright © 2009 by Cliff Lee

THE ALLIS FAMILY. Mr. and Mrs. Allis lived away out West, on a broad prairie, where Mr. Allis was busily engaged in "making a farm." Perhaps some of my young readers, who have always been accustomed to see farms already "made," will not understand what I mean by "making a farm;" and I will try to tell them.

First of all, let them try to fancy a large meadow, either perfectly flat or a little uneven, as large, perhaps, as can be measured with the eye, and sometimes without a single tree, or scarcely a clump of bushes. There will be no fences in sight, and sometimes no streams of water, but the surface of the ground is covered with high, coarse grass. This is what Western people call a "prairie."

In order to "make a farm," this ground must be ploughed, or, as Western people say, "broken up." Some of the children would smile, I think, if they were to see a regular "breaking team" before a "breaking plough." This plough is quite unlike that which is used in the older States, and it takes five, six, and sometimes as many as eight yoke of oxen to draw it. This ploughing is usually done in June. After ploughing, the ground must be enclosed, and then it is ready for the seed.

Some people make curious mistakes when they undertake to make a new farm. Mr. Allis was one of these persons. He arrived at the little town of B——, with his family, late in the fall, and immediately set about looking for a location. Several miles from B—— he found a place that seemed to suit him. The soil was rich, and apparently inexhaustible; but it was poorly watered, and destitute of any timber suitable for building or fencing, and there was very little which was fit for fuel. The great thing he thought of was a large farm.

After a while he found out his mistake, but it was too late for him to help it, for his money was nearly all expended for land. But Mr. Allis was a resolute man, and he immediately set himself to work to do the best he could. It was a long walk to the grove where he went every day to cut down trees for his cabin, and to split rails for his fence, and a whole day's work to go twice with his oxen to draw the logs and rails to his farm. But he rose early, and was ready to begin his work with the dawn. On rainy and stormy days, when he could not be out, he was at work in a shop near his house, making doors and window-frames, and cupboards, and other things for his new house.

Early in the spring the cabin was reared, and soon all was in readiness for the removal of the family, which consisted of Mrs. Allis, Mary, a distant relative whose home was with her, and two little twin-daughters, Annie and Susie, who were about five years old at this time. These little girls loved each other very much, and usually played very pleasantly together. But it was sometimes the case that, like other children, they had their little troubles, and were selfish, and of course unhappy.

One day Mrs. Allis was very sick, and she called the little girls to her, and told them they might go up-stairs and play, but they must try to be very good girls, and very quiet, for she could not bear the noise of their voices. The little girls loved their mother very dearly, and were very sorry that she was so sick. So they promised to be good children, and then away they skipped up-stairs on tip-toe, that they might not disturb their mother.

At first there was the patter of light feet and a subdued murmur of voices, but after a while scarcely a sound could be heard. Thus passed two hours, or more, and at last Mrs. Allis sent Mary to see what they were about. Mary reported that they were playing very pleasantly together, and seemed very happy.

"But what can they be doing, Mary?"

"Oh, they have a whole regiment of ragbabies, besides the kittens, for scholars. Susie says they are playing school."

At last it was tea-time, and, when the girls had eaten their supper, their mother called them to her.

"Oh, mother! mother! we have had such a nice time."

"Softly, softly, children," said Mr. Allis; "be careful, or you will make your mother sick again."

"Are you better now, mother?" said little Susie, going softly towards her bed.

"Yes, my dear child, I am much better, and you two little girls have helped to make me so."

"We, mother?" said Susie, while her black eyes sparkled at the thought. "I wonder how we could make you better, when we have been all the while at play up-stairs."

"I can guess how," said Annie. "Mother means we didn't make any noise: don't you, mother?"

"Not just that, or rather a good deal more than that; but first tell me what you played up-stairs."

"Oh, it was so pleasant: wasn't it? Why, mother, don't you think, we played school; and first I let Susie be teacher, and then she let me; and we played I was a little girl come to school, and by-and-by, when we got tired of that, we got out the dolls, Bessie and Jessie, and the pussy, and then we made three more little girls out of our sun-bonnets and Susie's pink apron, and then we both played teacher, like Miss Jackson and Miss Williams in the academy where we used to live, you know."

"Oh, yes, mother," interrupted Susie; "and, don't you think, sometimes Annie would pull pussy's tail and make her say 'Mew,' and we made believe that one of the little girls cried to go to her mother."

"Yes," said Annie, "and after a while we made believe she was naughty, and sent her home."

"Very well, my dear; I see you have had a very pleasant time,—much more pleasant than if you had been cross and unkind to each other, or had made a noise to disturb me. I see you have loved one another, and this is what has made you so happy this afternoon. Tell me, now, which you had rather be, teacher or scholar, when you play school."

"Oh! a teacher, a great deal, mother," said Annie.

"Then why did you not be teacher all the time, and let Susie be the scholar?"

"That wouldn't be right. Susie likes to be teacher as well as I," replied Annie, timidly.

"But don't you think you would have been happier to have been teacher all the time, Annie?"

"I did want to be at first, but then I thought Susie would like it too; and, after all, it was just as pleasant."

"I presume it was, my dear, and much more pleasant; no person can be happy who is selfish. Do you know what it is to be selfish, my little Susie?"

"Yes, mother; you told Annie and I one day that it was selfish to want every thing just to please ourselves."

"Do you love to run about the room, and laugh and play?"

"Oh, yes; you know we do, mother."

"Would you not rather have stayed down-stairs to play to-day?"

"Oh, yes," said Annie; "only——"

"Only what, my dear?"

"Annie means that you were sick, and didn't want us to make a noise; and, really, we did try to play just as still as we possibly could."

"Why did you take so much pains to be quiet?"

"You told us to be still, didn't you, mother?"

"I did; but were you afraid I would punish you if you made a noise, Susie?"

"Oh, no, indeed; but we did not want to make you sick," said Susie, clinging to her mother, and looking into her face with her loving eyes.

"Then you love your mother, do you, girls?"

"Indeed we do," said the children, in one breath.

"Well, supposing your mother had been well, and some poor sick woman, whom you had never seen before, lay here sick in my bed: would it have been more pleasant then for you to be very still, so as not to disturb her?"

The girls hesitated a moment, and then Annie said,—

"I think it would, mother; for it would be very cruel to make anybody suffer, I have heard you say."

"Then you could love a poor stranger enough to deny yourself some of your own pleasures for her sake; and you think it would make you happier to do so, do you?"

"Oh, yes, I am sure we should be happier," said little Susie.

"Well, my dear children, I cannot talk any longer now, but I want you to repeat this little verse after me until you can remember it:—

???"Love is the golden chain that binds    ??????"The happy souls above;    ????And he's an heir of heaven that finds    ??????His bosom glow with love."

\* \* \* \* \*

THE PRAIRIE FIRE. It was a trying summer for the Allis family. The weather was hot and dry, and Mr. Allis, unaccustomed to labour in the fields, often almost fainted in the sun. His work seemed to him to progress very slowly. He had no one to assist him in sowing and planting and gathering in his crops; for, in the first place, there were few people to be hired, and, more than that, he had no money to pay his workmen if he had been able to obtain them. Every morning he had to go more than a mile with his oxen for water, which he brought in a barrel for family use; and it was often nine o'clock before he got to his work in the fields.

At length November came and found his summer's work completed. He had no barn in which to store his grain, and could only secure it by "stacking" it until it could be threshed.

The potatoes, squashes, pumpkins, beets, turnips and other vegetables which the garden had produced for winter use were as securely housed as possible and protected from the frost; and Mr. Allis began to hope that now he might take that rest which he so much required.

For a number of weeks the children had been excited by wonderful lights in the sky, just above the horizon. Sometimes eight or ten of these could be seen in different directions at once, and occasionally some one of them would seem to shoot up suddenly, not unlike the flame of a distant volcano. To the eager inquiries of the little ones, they were answered that these singular lights were called prairie-fires.

"What is a prairie-fire, father?" asked both the children at once.

"It is the burning of the long coarse grass which covers the prairie in summer. This becomes very dry, and then, if a spark of fire chances to fall upon it, it is at once all in blaze."

"Does it make a very big fire, father?" asked Susie.

"That depends upon circumstances, my child. If the grass is very high and thick, as it sometimes is in the sloughs and moist places, it makes a big fire, as you call it."

"Oh, how I wish I could see a prairie-fire close by us! Don't you, mother?"

"I cannot say that I do, my child; they are sometimes rather mischievous visitors, and I would much prefer that they should keep at a respectful distance."

"Mr. Jenkins told me that a man some ten miles from here had his stacks and house and every thing he had, destroyed, a few days since, losing his whole year's labour and all his clothing and furniture. The family barely escaped with their lives.

"Is there any danger that the fire will come here, husband?" said Mrs. Allis.

"There is danger, I suppose; but I hope we shall have no trouble of that kind."

"Is there nothing that can be done to protect your property?"

"I shall try to burn up what grows around the house and stack-yard in a day or two, I think; but just now it does not seem possible for me to spare the time."

One day, not long after, a long line of fire appeared on the prairie, several miles distant. It was, however, so distant that Mrs. Allis and the children did not feel alarmed, as the evening was still; and they were watching it with interest, as the flames assumed various fantastic shapes, now darting upwards like tongues of fire, and now weltering and bubbling like a sea of melted lava. Mr. Allis had not yet returned from town, where he had been engaged all that day, entirely unsuspicious of any approaching calamity; and Mrs. Allis was not aware how rapidly the flames were approaching her home, until she was startled by seeing a horseman ride rapidly to her door and hastily dismount, inquiring for Mr. Allis.

"He is at ———. I expect him home in the course of an hour or so. But what is the matter, Mr. Jenkins? Is anybody sick?"

"Matter, woman! Don't you see that prairie-fire yonder? You'll be burnt out if you don't stir round lively."

"Burnt out, Mr. Jenkins! What do you mean? What shall we do?"

"Do? Why, we must go to work right away and set a back-fire,— as quick as we can, too. Call your girl there, and come out both of you as soon as possible!"

Not many minutes passed before Mr. Allis reached home. He had seen the fire at a distance, and, understanding the danger far better than his wife, hurried home as rapidly as possible.

Poor Annie and Susie were sadly frightened. When they saw the smoke and fire so near the house and stacks of grain, they cried as if their little hearts would break; but there was no one to hear them, for their mother could not be spared a moment until the danger was past. Poor children! They soon had enough of prairie-fires, and they thought they would be very thankful if ever they could see their father and mother and Mary alive again. Sometimes they were almost suffocated by the smoke which the rising wind drove into the house, and then they thought they should surely be burned to death. Still, lonely and frightened as they were, they did not attempt to go out. They remembered that their mother had told them not on any account to leave the house, and, like obedient children, they did as she had told them.

It was two hours—but it seemed much longer to the poor little girls— before their mother came in; and then they scarcely knew her, for her face was blackened with smoke and dust, her hands were burned sadly, and the skirt of her dress torn and burned in many places. Although they were excited and curious, yet these good children undressed and went to bed, helping themselves all they could, that their mother might rest, and trying to wait until morning for all they wished to know.

Meanwhile, Mrs. Allis busied herself, weary as she was, in providing a comfortable supper for her husband, who had eaten nothing since dinner-time. It was past midnight when Mr. Allis and Mary came to the house, and they too were tired enough, as we may suppose.

But, above all, they were grateful to that kind heavenly Father who had so mercifully preserved and protected them from harm amid such dangers. Little did any of them sleep that night; and it was not strange that the morning, which came on wet and showery, found them but little refreshed after the unusual fatigue of the preceding night. But the children were awake with the first light, and eagerly asking questions about the fire.

"But what is a back-fire?" said Annie, when her father had finished telling them about the matter. "How do you set a back-fire?"

"Well, Annie, we light another fire, nearer the house or fence which we are trying to save, and then, with a brush or broom, or sometimes a little stick, whip it out, so that it cannot burn very fast. When the grass is burnt off in this way there is nothing left for what we call the 'prairie-fire' to burn, you see. If we can do this in season, the house or stacks are generally safe."

\* \* \* \* \*

THE BABY. How tired every one was all day after the prairie-fire! Well would it have been if the matter had terminated in fatigue. Early in the day the feeble mother had to betake herself to her bed; and on the following morning Mr. Allis, to his great surprise, found himself rudely shaken by the ague. Not many days passed ere Mrs. Allis and Mary found themselves at the mercy of the same annoying visitor. Sometimes the three shook in concert; and then you may imagine that the little girls had enough to do to carry water to satisfy their thirst. Occasionally the chills would seem to be broken up for a few days, and then they would most unexpectedly return. Several times Mr. Allis thought himself perfectly well, and once or twice he went to the grove a number of miles distant, with his team, for a load of wood, and on the way there or back would be attacked with a chill, and it was only by a great effort that he reached home. The little girls were quite well; but they did not find their prairie home as pleasant in the cold winter as it was in the glad summer-time. Oh, how they longed for spring! And when it came how they rejoiced over the little lambs and calves in their father's yard, and how delighted were they when the first sweet violets peeped forth! Still their joy was to be increased: a sweeter prairie-flower than any of these bloomed in their humble cabin, opening a fount of untold gladness in the hearts of all. One bright morning a sweet little sister was presented to the delighted children.

It was long before they could be made to realize that it was their own dear babe, and always to be theirs and to stay with them. At last they recovered themselves sufficiently to ask its name.

"It has no name, Annie," said her father.

"Oh, mother! mother!" cried the enthusiastic Susie, "let us call it Love!"

What a blessing that little unconscious one was to all beneath that lowly roof! Annie and Susie would sit beside its little cradle and watch it for hours; and if permitted to hold the tiny creature for a few moments they were never weary of caressing her. Daily and almost hourly they discovered some new beauty or perfection in the dear object of their most tender regard, and the day of her birth was made an era in the house; for almost every thing that was spoken of was said to have taken place either so long before or so long after the Baby came.

At length a school was opened about a mile distant, and the parents thought best that the little girls should have the advantage of attending it through the summer. At first they were quite reluctant to go; for they were strangers still to the children around them, and the young lady who taught them they had never seen until they met her among her pupils. After a few days they became very fond of their school and their young playmates, and the only drawback to their happiness was leaving the little darling Mary for so many long hours every day. But it was soon evident that they learned some evil things as well as good things. They grew less willing to submit to the gentle control of their parents, and were quite inclined to think the rules under whose influence they had been educated were altogether too strict, fortifying their occasional remonstrances with "Mary Jones says so," or "Fanny Adams thinks so." This gave their affectionate parents much solicitude and pain.

One evening the little girls came home with a petition that they might "go to school barefooted," and, as usual for the last few weeks, Susie said, "All the girls go without shoes."

"That, my child, is no reason why you should do so if we prefer you should wear your shoes."

"But, mother, it is so warm!" said Annie.

"What would you have thought, Annie, if I had told you to go to school barefooted while we lived in Massachusetts?"

"All the girls wore shoes and stockings there, mother."

"But was it not quite as warm there as here, my child?"

"I suppose so; but, mother, all the girls and boys laugh at us so. They say we are 'proud,' because we wear shoes and stockings."

"You must not mind being laughed at when you are doing right."

"But I can't see what wrong there is in going barefooted," said Annie.

"You are not now required to see the harm in it. All you have to do in this case is to obey."

"But won't you tell us why, mother?" persisted Susie.

"No, children, I shall not now tell you why. I have my reasons; and you must trust me now, and wait for an explanation until some future time."

\* \* \* \* \*

ANNIE'S TEMPTATION. A few days after, Susie was not very well, and her mother thought best to keep her at home. Annie, however, was sent to school, as usual. As she was preparing to set out, she thought to herself,—

"Now I am going all alone, and mother will never know it; I will not wear my shoes to-day." So, when she was just starting, she stole softly round to the back-side of the house, and hid her shoes behind the rain-barrel. On she skipped, but not so light-hearted and happy as usual. It was her first act of wilful disobedience. As she went on she at last repented that she had ventured to disobey her kind mother; but something seemed to whisper in her heart, "It will do you no harm: your mother will never find it out."

Do any of my little readers know whose voice that was in Annie's heart? It was the voice of him who spoke the first lie ever uttered in this beautiful world; who in the garden of Eden said to our first mother, "Ye shall not surely die."

As she approached the school-room, she stopped near a huge pile of rocks at the road-side to gather some flowers for her teacher. She found a great many, and, among others, some which she had never seen before. As she stooped forward hastily to pluck them, she heard a sound close by her. Looking quickly about her, she spied a large snake just below her naked feet, among the loose stones. Uttering a loud scream, she sprang terrified from the spot; nor did she slacken her speed until she reached the schoolhouse, her delicate feet cut and bleeding in several places, and a large thorn in the side of one foot, which pained her sadly. The girls laughed at her fright, and one rude boy ran out, shouting, at the top of his voice,—

"Hallo, boys! hallo! Annie Allis has come to school barefooted."

Poor, foolish child! what would she have given if she had only obeyed her mother!

The little white feet swelled and ached all the day long. Annie had hardly ever felt so much pain in all her life, and there was nobody to pity her. But the pain in her feet was nothing to the pain in her heart. How could she meet her dear mother, after having so wickedly disobeyed her? At length school was out. Slowly and painfully she walked homeward. As she approached the house she shook with pain and dread. Down in the little grove at her right hand she saw Susie and Mary with the dear little baby, and they beckoned her to come to them; but she could not. Oh, how could the guilty child look into the clear, sweet eyes of that innocent one, with such a load of sin and disobedience on her heart?

Softly—just like a thief—she stole round the house, as she thought, unobserved. She sat down on the little green mound beside the rain-barrel, and reached behind it. Suddenly she started back as if a serpent had stung her. Again she reached quite around the barrel, as far as she could stretch her little arms; but nothing was there. Then she peered carefully into the place; but no shoes were to be found. It is plain now,—quite plain. What shall be done? Some one has taken the shoes away! Overpowered entirely, she bursts into a passionate fit of crying. Who is it that approaches the erring child and so kindly and tenderly inquires,—

"What is the matter, Annie?"

It is the mother, weary as she can be, and made still more weary and sorrowful by her little daughter's disobedience. She takes the child into the house and lays her upon the bed. The aching feet are bathed in water, the dirt is washed from the scratches and wounds, while poor Annie weeps and sobs as if her little heart would break. But the ugly thorn would not come out: it must ache on until father comes. Silently and sadly the mother bends over her suffering child, bathing her aching head. At length Annie said,—

"Dear, dear mother, forgive me; and I will never, never want to disobey you again!"

I suppose every child knows just what this good Christian mother said to her little unhappy daughter,—how she told her that she had offended God as well as her mother, and broken his good law. She told her, too, how sinful it was to try to deceive, and then comforted her with her full and free pardon, and said that her heavenly Father would pardon her even more freely than her mother did, if she truly repented of her fault and asked his forgiveness with her whole heart. Then she taught Annie to pray,

"Lead me not into temptation, but deliver me from evil;" and, although the little one had said that prayer many times, never, never had she understood its meaning so perfectly before: now she felt her dependence on God.

Soon Susie and Mary came in with the baby; and, while they were pitying poor Annie and asking questions, they placed the child on the bed beside her. There it laughed and crowed merrily and stretched out its little dimpled hands, while Annie, unable to smile in return, wondered how it could be so happy when she was so wretched.

It was late when Mr. Allis came in; and upon examining the foot he said the thorn would have to be cut out in the morning. In vain a soothing poultice was applied to the wound. Annie scarcely closed her eyes all night. Worse than that: she kept her mother awake, although she tried hard to be patient and bear the pain as well as she could. In the morning her father sharpened his penknife and cut out the thorn. Of course he was very careful, but it did hurt sadly. It was many days before the poor foot got well; and I think Annie Allis will remember her mother's "reasons" for refusing to go without her shoes for many a day.

\* \* \* \* \*

SUSIE'S TEMPTATION.   No sooner had Annie and Susie made acquaintance with some of the children in the neighbourhood than they began to make frequent visits at Mr. Allis's house. Both father and mother thought it desirable that the little girls should associate with other children; but they dreaded the effect of so much society and so many new influences on the hearts of the little girls. More than this: there were some among those that visited them frequently, who seemed to be almost any thing but desirable companions for the children. Once or twice Mrs. Allis had observed something in the manners and conversation of Jane Smith which led her to suspect that she was a bad girl. Accordingly, she told Annie and Susie that she wished they would, as much as possible, avoid her society. Notwithstanding all she could say, however, Jane was often at the house; and the children became very fond of her. She could tell so many interesting stories and say so many witty things, and had so much to communicate that was new to them, that they seemed almost fascinated by her.

One Saturday afternoon Mrs. Allis was unusually busy, and Jane came to pay another visit. In spite of her cares, she, however, contrived to find amusement for the girls in her own presence. After tea, Jane took her bonnet to go home, and Susie begged permission to walk a short distance with her, to gather prairie-flowers. Mrs. Allis hesitated, but at length gave her consent, specifying the distance which she might go.

Scarcely had they started on their walk, when Jane remarked,—

"I declare! it's mean in your mother to keep you so dreadful close, just as though you didn't know enough to take care of yourself!"

"Mother isn't mean; and you must not say so, Jane, or I shall go right home."

"What! You're mad, are you? Well, I'm sure I don't care, if you don't; but I'm glad my mother don't do so, anyway!"

Susie now turned the conversation, and told Jane that Miss Wilson was making new bonnets for her and Annie. After some questions as to what kind of bonnets they were, and how they were trimmed, Jane asked,—

"When are they going to be done?"

"I suppose they are done to-day; but we shall not get them until some time next week, for it is too late for father to go to-night, and he is very tired besides."

"Why don't you go and get them yourself? I would."

"Oh, it's too far to go."

"Nonsense! It's only two miles."

"But mother did not send me: she would have sent me if she had wished me to go."

"Pooh! she thought you would be afraid to go! I'll warrant she would be glad enough to see the bonnets home. Come along, now! I'll go with you. You know you can't go to meeting tomorrow if you don't get your bonnet."

"Oh, yes: we can wear our clean sun-bonnets."

"Wear your sun-bonnet to meeting! I'd stay at home first!"

"I wouldn't stay at home first! But I would like a new bonnet, too. I would go and get it if I thought mother would like it."

"Like it! why, to-be-sure she will! Come along."

With hesitating steps Susie went on. Just before her was the point which her mother had made the limit of her walk. She felt no desire to disobey her mother; but the thought of surprising her by bringing home the new bonnets unexpectedly was quite a temptation. Then it would be so pleasant to have them, too; she wanted to see how they looked very much indeed. Why could she not walk very fast and get back soon? She looked at the sun, to see how much time there would be. It was almost setting; and she exclaimed,—

"Jane! I can't go! See; it is almost sundown!"

"It will be light for two hours. There is time enough; we can run, and get back before dark."

"What if I shouldn't get the bonnets after all? What would mother say?"

"You'll get them fast enough; and, even if you don't, you needn't tell her. She'll never know it! Come along!"

Jane had said one word too many now. The frightened child had done the best thing she could have done. The idea of deceiving her mother had put the matter in an entirely new light, and she ran homeward, without one word of reply, as fast as her little feet could carry her. As soon as she reached the house she told the story to Annie and Mary, through whom it soon reached the mother's ears. She had no more occasion to caution her little girls to avoid Jane Smith.

"How much our mother knows! Don't she, Susie?" said Annie; "she told us long ago that Jane was a naughty girl; but we didn't see how it could be!"

\* \* \* \* \*

THE COLD DAY    Both Susie and Annie Allis had learned a good lesson, and both of them profited by it. They found, each for herself, how much safer and better it was to trust their parents and obey their commands, whether they understood all about them or not. These kind parents often reminded their little ones that their good Father in heaven knew just what kind of parents he had given the children, and that he required them to yield a willing and cheerful obedience to all their parents' will, unless their commands involved the breaking of his holy law. That this would be the case the little girls did not fear, and, taught, as we believe, by the good Spirit from above, they tried very hard to please God by honouring their parents.

The winter was quite mild and pleasant, and Mrs. Allis thought best that Annie and Susie should continue to attend school as long as the weather would permit. It was a long walk for little girls not quite seven years old; but when the sky was bright and the path good they did not mind the cold air, for they were warmly clad and full of health and animation; they ran gayly along, scarcely heeding the distance they had to go.

One morning Mr. and Mrs. Allis had occasion to go to a neighbouring town on business, and Mary was left at home alone with the baby. The children rode to school with their parents, and, when they got out of the wagon at the door of the log school-house, Annie said,—

"Will you get back before night, father?"

"Probably not. If we do we will call and take you home."

The morning was somewhat dark and cloudy, and a dense fog settled in the hollows and ravines. Towards noon, however, there was a change; a cold north wind began to blow, as it blows nowhere except on the wide open prairies, unless it be on the sea. The clouds soon disappeared and the bright sun shone out clear and bright. Every hour the cold increased, until it became intense. The school-mistress dismissed the children somewhat earlier than usual and called them all around the huge fireplace to warm themselves. Then, after she had carefully fastened their cloaks and tippets and charged them to run home as fast as they could, they started out.

Poor little Annie and Susie had to go alone. None of the children lived in the direction of their home; and, worse than all, they had the cold, fierce wind directly in their faces. But they thought of no danger while the sun was shining so brightly; and so on they went, running backwards to keep the wind out of their faces. Somewhat more than half-way home, a little aside from the road, lived a family by the name of Staunton. When they were just opposite to the house they found themselves very cold.

"Oh, Annie! do let's go in and warm, ourselves," said Susie; "I am so cold!"

"I can't stop, Susie," said Annie; "don't you know mother said we mustn't stop on the way home from school?"

"Well, I don't think mother would care if we stopped now; I am so very cold. Do you?"

"I don't know; I guess we had better hurry home as fast as we can. It would be hard work to start again, you know."

At this juncture the wind tore away Annie's cloak, and the little girls forgot their cold hands as they chased it away off towards the pile of rocks where Annie saw the snake in the summer. Under the shelter of those rocks they sat down a moment to put on the cloak. Of course, mittens must be laid aside, and the little, stiff, benumbed fingers had hard work to fasten the garment, which had lost one of its strings in the encounter with the rude north wind. When at last it was made fast with a pin, Susie said,—

"I am going to rub my hands with snow, Annie! You know Dick Matthews said that he could warm his hands with snow when they were cold!"

Both the little ones rubbed their hands with the snow, and again set out, holding each other firmly by the hand. Several times they repeated the experiment, baring the little delicate fingers to the biting wind. At last they ceased to ache; but the feet were stiff and their limbs tired and weary.

"Do your hands ache now, Susie?"

"No; but my feet do, and my face. Oh, I'm afraid we'll never get home! a'n't you, Annie?"

"It's hard work to walk, and I can hardly stir one step;" when I turn my back it seems as if I should fall right down. I do wish Mary would come down to the field and open the gate! don't you?"

"Yes, I do; for my hands are just as stiff as they can be."

"There come father and mother, Annie; let's wait and ride," said Susie.

"We'd better go and open the gate. See! there comes Mary! A'n't you glad?"

"I can't stay for any thing; I shall run right to the fire! My feet are freezing, almost," said Susie.

At that moment Mary came. She had been watching for the children, and as soon as they came in sight she laid down the baby and ran to help them come in the house. She set the gate wide open for the wagon, and then hurried the girls in to the fire. Soon the parents came in.

"How glad we are to see you, children! We were almost afraid you would be frozen. We tried to get home in time to take you in the wagon. Are not your hands very cold?"

"Our feet are cold; our hands were, too, but they are not now."

"Not now?" said Mary, hastily drawing off Annie's mittens.

Alas! the little fingers were frozen! Susie's were in the same sad condition. And now there was a brisk rubbing with snow, and the most intense suffering as the slow-coming warmth returned to the purple hands.

"Annie," said Mr. Allis, when the pain of the hands was somewhat relieved, "why did you not stop at Mr. Staunton's and warm yourself?"

"Because, father," said Annie, looking up meekly through her tears, "mother has told us never to stop on our way home from school, and I always try to mind what she tells us now!"

THE END.

www.ingramcontent.com/pod-product-compliance
Lightning Source LLC
Chambersburg PA
CBHW071322280526
45788CB00004B/1988